Monday Morning Inspiration

THE FIRST BURST OF **ENERGY** BASED ON *SCRIPTURES* TO START A NEW WEEK

DR. WILLIE J. THOMPSON JR.

DEDICATIONS

To those who still find value in reading books, meditating, reflecting and journaling…

The Kingdoms Of This World Are Yours.

FOREWORD BY CECIL POSTELL

As we go from day to day through life's journey, there comes a time when we need some spiritual enlightening to help us make it through the week. From Tuesday through Thursday, we focus on going to work to get the needed money to make ends meet, knowing that Friday and Saturday are coming, and we can't wait to turn up in any manner we deem necessary.

Then comes Sunday, a day that we feel the need to venture into the church and give the Lord a little something and get back a blessing to help us make it through the week. The Word comes forth as taught and explained by the servant of God and we are pumped and filled with what we feel is power from on high. A power that had us rocking and reeling until we depart through the doors of the sanctuary.

That same afternoon, life hits us in the face with a reality uppercut, and the seed we swallowed early Sunday morning has seemingly vanished into thin air. What is one to do as we go to sleep, hoping that things will change come Monday morning? We wake up waddling in the need of a Monday Morning Inspiration, to which I can attest, that help has arrived. Pastor Willie J. has been given an assignment by God to help you fulfill the need in the form of an inspirational book.

This book of Monday Morning Inspiration was a vision
inscribed in his heart,
to help us as mankind receive a divine, weekly, needed, spiritual start,
that will help to ignite a fire that is fueled and burning throughout
the week.

So, I invite you to indulge in this book of inspiration as the Holy
Spirit speaks.

This Monday Morning Inspiration that I bring to you,
will help you to acknowledge what God wants you to do,
after Sunday morning service, in which you received spiritual
nourishment,
that seemed to have vanished and left you in a place of
discouragement.

All the while, life issues, and mishaps affront you face to face,
with unwanted conflicts you wholeheartedly do not want to embrace.
What can I do, is the question that seemingly arises,
as the adversary throws forth many blows of compromises.

Where can I turn to find some kind of spiritual motivation,
come on and join in reading this Monday Morning Inspiration.
Fifty-two weeks of Spirit-filled declarations.
that will help us to avoid a life of total damnation.

No need to worry, nor do you have to look any further,
these Words transcribed from above will act as life preserver.
To help you with instruction on how to make it through the week,
the Word from the Lord in which we must all continually seek.

Thank you, Pastor Wille J. Thompson,
for heeding what God gave you and not turning away,
These words from your Monday Morning Inspiration,
will help souls to not go astray.

The Lord gave you a plan and you fulfilled your part,
Now let's hope that the people will take this to heart.

This book of Monday Morning Inspiration is something that I pray will bless each of you and allow you to read, to fellowship and become one with the Lord.

1

Good Morning!

As we have crossed over into a new year, let us remember that 'We live within the shadow of the Almighty, sheltered by the God who is above all gods. This I declare that he alone is my refuge, my place of safety; he is my God, and I am trusting him. For he rescues you from every trap and protects you from the fatal plague. He will shield you with his wings! They will shelter you. His faithful promises are your armor. Now you don't need to be afraid of the dark anymore, nor fear the dangers of the day; nor dread the plagues of darkness, nor disasters in the morning!

This is our Monday Morning Inspiration. We are determined to have a Great Week but also a Great Year!

Favor Be Upon You!

Dr. Willie, David the Psalmist, and Our God: Our Buckler and Shield!

Scripture References:

Psalm 91:1 - 6

Psalm 91:14 -16

Let's Write!:

Reflect on a time when you felt God's protection and refuge in your life. How did this experience impact your trust in Him?

____

____

____

____

____

____

How can you apply the promises of God's protection and provision in Psalm 91 to your daily life and challenges this year?

____

____

____

____

____

____

2

Good Morning!

We are holding strong to the momentum of this new year, and while some things may seem more challenging than they really are, take courage. You have an Ever-Present Helper. And the way you activate Him is simply by taking your hand, gently tapping, and reminding someone else that Help is this close!

Alone, it may look impossible, BUT DON'T WORRY... YOU ARE NOT ALONE! And with God, All Things are POSSIBLE.

This is our Monday Morning Inspiration! Have A Great Week!

Baby Brother Dr. Willie, Brother Dr. Luke, Brother Apostle Paul, Big Brother Jesus Christ, and Invisible Brother/Sister Holy Ghost.

Scripture References:

Matthew 19:26

Philippians 4:13

LET'S WRITE!:

Reflect on a time when you experienced God's help or presence in a challenging situation. How did it impact your perspective on difficulties?

____

____

____

____

____

____

____

How can you be an instrument of God's help and encouragement to others this week, especially during challenging times?

____

____

____

____

____

3

Good Morning!

Let me share this joy with you! "I'm thanking you, God, from a full heart, I'm writing the book on your wonders. I'm whistling, laughing, and jumping for joy; I'm singing your song, High God. The day my enemies turned tail and ran, they stumbled on you and fell on their faces. God took over and set everything right; when I needed you, you were there, taking charge. God holds the high center, God's a safe house for the battered, a sanctuary during bad times. Sing your songs to Zion-dwelling God, tell his stories to everyone you meet!"

This is Our Monday Morning Inspiration. Let's go and have a Great Week!

Dr. Willie, The Psalmist, God our Defender, and Vindicator!

Scripture References:

Psalm 9:1-2

Psalm 18:2

Let's Write!:

Reflect on a time when you experienced God's intervention in a challenging situation. How did it impact your faith and perspective?

____

____

____

____

____

____

How can you share the stories of God's faithfulness and protection with those around you this week?

____

____

____

____

____

Good Morning!

Apostle Paul rises to remind us that "When we are in Christ, we are new creatures." And God has done the work of reconciling our relationship with Him. And now we have the ambassadorial role of going out and convincing others to drop their differences with God and others. For God and others (in Christ) have already dropped their differences with you! We are ministers and agents of reconciliation! It's time to clock in!

This is our Monday Morning Inspiration. Let's have a great week! And base that greatness off of how many people we can get to BE RECONCILED! Let's Go!!!

Dr. Willie, Apostle Paul, 2nd Cor. 5 and The God who has nothing against you and wants you to have nothing against each other!

Scripture References:

2 Corinthians 5:17-20

Matthew 5:23-24

Let's Write!:

Reflect on a time when you experienced reconciliation in a relationship. How did it impact your life and your understanding of God's grace?

____

____

____

____

____

____

How can you actively participate in the ministry of reconciliation in your daily interactions and relationships this week?

____

____

____

____

____

5

Good Morning!

The Gospel Writer John rises to remind us that: "Anyone who accepts God and Anyone Who Believes God, will become the children of God and get a fresh start in Him." So, if you simply lean in and put your weight on Him, You get a fresh start!

This is Our Monday Morning Inspiration. Let's Have A Great Week!

Dr. Willie, John 1 and The Light of the World!

Scripture References:

John 1:12-13

John 3:16

Let's Write!:

Reflect on a time when you experienced the transformative power of accepting and believing in God's love and grace. How did it impact your life and relationships?

____

____

____

____

____

____

What steps can you take this week to lean into God and experience a fresh start in Him?

____

____

____

____

____

6

Good Morning!

The Apostle Paul rises this morning to exhort us to consider our associations/networks/the folk we hang with, with these words: "Don't fool yourselves. Bad friends will destroy you."

This is our simple, sweet, and strong Monday Morning Inspiration. Now let's go out there and have a great week!

Dr. Willie, Apostle Paul, The People of 1st Corinthians 15 and The One Who helps us to discern all things even though we sometimes don't want to listen (Holy Ghost).

Scripture References:

1 Corinthians 15:33

Proverbs 13:20

Let's Write!:

Reflect on the influence of your friendships and associations on your life and decisions. How do they impact your spiritual growth and well-being?

____

____

____

____

____

____

____

Are there any relationships in your life that you need to reevaluate or possibly distance yourself from for the sake of your spiritual health? If so, what steps can you take to address this?

____

____

____

____

____

____

7

Good Morning!

We have many things to thank God for. And Apostle Paul shares with us, "And here's what He's done: He has graced us and sanctioned us as His emissaries whose mission is to spread the one true and obedient faith to all people in the name of Jesus." This includes you: you have been called by Jesus, God's Anointed.

Let's take this Word and Have A Great Week!

Dr. Willie, Apostle Paul, Romans 1, The Pilgrims to Athens, The Lord Jesus Christ and The Holy Ghost and Wind of God.

Scripture References:

Romans 1:5

Acts 17:16

Let's Write!:

Reflect on the significance of being called by Jesus to spread the faith. How does this call impact your sense of purpose and identity?

____

____

____

____

____

____

How can you actively fulfill your role as an emissary of the one true faith in your daily life and interactions with others this week?

____

____

____

____

____

____

8

Good Morning!

The Apostle Paul's letter to the church at Philippi rises to encourage us with these words: "I am confident that the Creator (The One that brings all things into existence), who has begun such a great work among you, will not stop in mid-design but will keep perfecting you until the day Jesus the Anointed, our Liberating King, returns to redeem the world."

God is at work in you and all around you!!! Keep Going! God is Not Through Yet!

Now this IS OUR MONDAY MORNING INSPIRATION! Let's have a Great Week!

Dr. Willie, Philippians 1, and The Creator, Writer, Designer and Author of Your Life...

Scripture References:

Philippians 1:6

1 Thessalonians 5:24

Let's Write!:

Reflect on the assurance that God is continually at work in your life, perfecting and shaping you for His purposes. How does this truth encourage you in your journey of faith?

____

____

____

____

____

____

____

In what areas of your life do you sense God is currently at work, refining and molding you? How can you cooperate with His work in these areas?

____

____

____

____

____

Good Morning!

The Word of the Lord to Joshua rises to speak with us today: "Have I not commanded you? Be strong and courageous. Do not be frightened, and do not be dismayed, for the Lord your God is with you wherever you go." Yep, God said, "wherever!" God is there in any season and any circumstance. God is with you in places you choose, and, in the places, God led you... do not be afraid... God is right there.

This is our Monday Morning Inspiration! Let's have a great week!

Dr. Willie, Joshua 1, The flame of Courage and Fire of the Holy Ghost!

Scripture References:

Joshua 1:9

Deuteronomy 31:6

Let's Write!:

Reflect on a time when you felt God's presence and courage in a challenging situation. How did His presence impact your response to the circumstance?

____

____

____

____

____

____

How can you cultivate a deeper awareness of God's presence in your daily life, especially in moments of fear or uncertainty?

____

____

____

____

____

Good Morning!

Moses rises to instruct us with these words: "Don't pervert justice. Don't show favoritism to either the poor or the great. Judge on the basis of what is right. "Don't spread gossip and rumors. "Don't just stand by when your neighbor's life is in danger. I am God. "Don't secretly hate your neighbor. If you have something against him, get it out into the open; otherwise, you are an accomplice in his guilt. "Don't seek revenge or carry a grudge against any of your people. "Love your neighbor as yourself. I am God!"

This is our Monday Morning Inspiration, now Let's Have A Great Week! I AM said So!

Dr. Willie, The Great I AM, Moses, The Children of God, and The Heavenly Hosts!

Scripture References:

Leviticus 19:15

Leviticus 19:18

Let's Write!:

Reflect on Moses' instructions regarding justice, gossip, and love for one's neighbor. How can you apply these principles in your interactions with others?

____

____

____

____

____

____

____

Is there any area in your life where you need to reconcile with a neighbor or release feelings of hatred or resentment? How can you take steps toward forgiveness and love this week?

____

____

____

____

____

____

Good Morning!

Let's join David in these words: "The Lord is my light and my salvation; whom shall, I fear? The Lord is the strength of my life; of whom shall I be afraid? When the wicked, even mine enemies and my foes, came upon me to eat up my flesh, they stumbled and fell. Though an host should encamp against me, my heart shall not fear: though war should rise against me, in this will I be confident. One thing have I desired of the Lord, that will I seek after; that I may dwell in the house of the Lord all the days of my life, to behold the beauty of the Lord, and to enquire in his temple. For in the time of trouble he shall hide me in his pavilion: in the secret of his tabernacle shall he hide me; he shall set me up upon a rock."

This is Our Monday Morning Inspiration and Great News for the start of a new week. Have a Great One!

Dr. Willie, David the Psalmist, Psalm 27, and The Lord of Hosts!

Scripture References:

Psalm 27:1-5

Psalm 46:1-3

Let's Write!:

Reflect on the assurance of God's protection and presence as expressed in Psalm 27. How does this assurance impact your outlook on life's challenges?

____

____

____

____

____

____

____

What can you do this week to cultivate a deeper desire to dwell in the presence of the Lord and seek His beauty and guidance in your life?

____

____

____

____

____

____

12

Good Morning!

The Apostle Paul rises to encourage us with these words: "Use your freedom to serve one another in love; that's how freedom grows. For everything we know about God's Word is summed up in a single sentence: Love others as you love yourself. That's an act of true freedom."

This is Our Monday Morning Inspiration! Let's have a great week!

Dr. Willie, Paul, The Saints at Galatia, and The Heavenly Host!

Scripture References:

Galatians 5:13-14

1 Peter 4:10

Let's Write!:

Reflect on the concept of using freedom to serve others in love as a manifestation of true freedom. How can you apply this principle in your daily life?

Consider a recent situation where you had the opportunity to serve someone in love. How did it impact you and the person you served? What did you learn from the experience?

13

Good Morning!

Moses rises to share with the Children of God, who are on the brink of a manifested promise these words: "Reverently respect God, your God, serve him, hold tight to him, back up your promises with the authority of his name. He Is Your Praise; He's your God! He did all these tremendous, these staggering things that you saw with your own eyes. When your ancestors entered Egypt, they numbered a mere seventy souls. And now look at you—you look more like the stars in the night skies in number. And your God did it."

This is great news to the start of a great new week. And This is Our Monday Morning Inspiration! Have a Great Week!

Dr. Willie, Moses, Deuteronomy 10, and all the Promise Manifesters!

Scripture References:

Deuteronomy 10:20-22

Genesis 15:5

LET'S WRITE!:

Reflect on the importance of reverently respecting and serving God as highlighted in Deuteronomy 10. How does this mindset impact your relationship with God?

____

____

____

____

____

____

____

Consider the promises God has fulfilled in your life. How do these experiences strengthen your faith and trust in Him for the future?

____

____

____

____

____

____

14

Good Morning!

The Apostle Paul rises to instruct us with these words shared with the believers at Colossae: "Be wise in the way you ·act with [behave towards] people who are not believers, making the most of every opportunity. When you talk, you should always be ·kind [gracious] and ·pleasant [winsome; engaging; or wholesome; seasoned with salt] so you will be able to answer everyone in the way you should."

This is our Monday Morning Inspiration and great words to start off a Great, Anointed and Eventful Week!

Dr. Willie, Apostle Paul, Colossians 4 and Our Great and Awesome God!

Scripture References:

Colossians 4:5-6

Ephesians 5:15-16

Let's Write!:

Reflect on the importance of being wise and gracious in our interactions with non-believers as instructed by Paul. How can you apply these principles in your daily life?

____

____

____

____

____

____

____

Think of a recent opportunity you had to engage with someone who doesn't share your faith. How did you handle the conversation? What could you do differently next time to be more effective in sharing your beliefs with kindness and grace?

____

____

____

____

____

Good Morning!

Many have asked, "how do you survive in such a challenging world?" Here's our response: "It takes more than bread to stay alive. It takes a steady stream of words from God's mouth."

Stay in the place that provides a steady stream of Words From God's Mouth! This is our Monday Morning Inspiration and the start of a great new week!

Bless You, My Friend!

Dr. Willie, Matthew 4 and the streams waiting for you!

Scripture References:

Matthew 4:4

Isaiah 55:2

Let's Write!:

Reflect on the importance of feeding on the words of God for spiritual nourishment and sustenance. How can you prioritize spending time in God's Word in your daily life?

____

____

____

____

____

____

Consider a time when you felt spiritually refreshed and strengthened by immersing yourself in Scripture. How did this experience impact your perspective and actions?

____

____

____

____

____

16

Good Morning!

I kept hearing in my ear change is coming! Deuteronomy 28:9 echoes this message with these words: "He will change you into a holy people dedicated to himself; this he has promised to do if you will only obey him and walk in his ways."

This is our Monday Morning Inspiration and Good News for the week ahead. Have a Great Week, My Friend!

Dr. Willie, Moses, and The Change That's On The Way!

Scripture References:

Deuteronomy 28:9

Romans 12:2

Let's Write!:

Reflect on the promise of transformation and change as described in Deuteronomy 28:9. How does obedience to God's commands play a role in this process?

____

____

____

____

____

____

Think about an area in your life where you desire to see change or growth. How can you align your actions and obedience with God's Word to facilitate transformation in that area?

____

____

____

____

____

____

Good Morning!

I want to encourage you that a CHANGE is On the way. God tells us in Isaiah 43:19, "See, I am doing a new thing! Now it springs up; do you not perceive it? I am making a way in the wilderness and streams in the wasteland."

This is Our Monday Morning Inspiration and Now Let's Go and Have a Great Week!

Dr. Willie, Isaiah The Prophet and The God Who Can Change Anything!

Scripture References:

Isaiah 43:19

2 Corinthians 5:17

LET'S WRITE!:

Reflect on the promise of new beginnings and change as described in Isaiah 43:19. How does this message bring hope and encouragement to your life?

____

____

____

____

____

____

____

Consider an area in your life where you long for God to do a new thing. How can you align your mindset and actions with God's promise to make a way and bring transformation in that area?

____

____

____

____

____

Good Morning!

May the words found in Genesis 24:15 follow you every day this week and beyond: "Before he had finished praying, Rebekah came out with her jar on her shoulder."

This is our Monday Morning Inspiration, now let's Have a Great Week!

Dr. Willie, Eliezer, Rebekah, and Our Manifest God.

Scripture References:

Genesis 24:15

Psalm 37:4

Let's Write!:

Reflect on the significance of God's timely answers to prayers as exemplified in Genesis 24:15. How does this encourage you to trust in God's provision and timing?

____

____

____

____

____

____

Think about a recent prayer request you've made to God. Have you seen any signs of His answer or provision? If not, how can you continue to trust and wait on Him this week?

____

____

____

____

____

____

Good Morning!

Some things in this life are unsure, unreliable, and undependable. But we can be assured that The God we serve is faithful to His Word.

Numbers 23 tells us: "God is not a man, that he should lie; neither the son of man, that he should repent: hath he said, and shall he not do it? or hath he spoken, and shall he not make it good?"

MUCH More than keep your ear to the ground, keep your ear towards God! Because if it is written and spoken that God will be your Buckler and Shield... it is written and forever will be written!

This is Our Monday Morning Inspiration. Now let's Have A Great Week!

Dr. Willie, The Unchanging Spoken and Written Word of God, and The Buckler and Shield!

Scripture References:

Numbers 23:19

Psalm 18:30

Let's Write!:

Reflect on the unchanging nature of God's Word and His faithfulness as described in Numbers 23:19. How does this truth impact your trust and confidence in God?

____

____

____

____

____

____

____

Think about a time when God proved Himself faithful to His promises in your life. How did this experience strengthen your faith and reliance on Him?

____

____

____

____

____

Good Morning!

Early the next morning they went out to the wilderness of Tekoa. There Jehoshaphat's message to Judah was not about courage in battle. But Jehoshaphat said: Listen to me, Judah, and inhabitants of Jerusalem. Trust in the Eternal One, your True God, not in your own abilities, and you will be supported. Put your trust in His words that you heard through the prophets, and we will succeed.

Let's Prophesy: "Believe in the Lord your God, so shall ye be established; believe his prophets, so shall ye prosper."

Prophesy! Believe firmly in God, your God, and your lives will be firm! Believe in your prophets and you'll come out on top!

This is Our Monday Morning Inspiration! Now let's walk in the strength of this Word and Have A Great Week!

Dr. Willie, 2 Chronicles 20, The Spirit of God, and Your Neighbor saying, "Prophesy!"

Scripture References:

2 Chronicles 20:20

Jeremiah 17:7-8

LET'S WRITE!:

Reflect on the importance of trusting in God's word and the role of prophecy in guiding our lives as illustrated in 2 Chronicles 20:20. How can you apply this principle in your decision-making process?

____

____

____

____

____

____

Consider a time when you experienced the fulfillment of a prophetic word or promise from God. How did this impact your faith and trust in Him?

____

____

____

____

____

21

Good Morning!

God can do anything, you know—far more than you could ever imagine or guess or request in your wildest dreams! He does it not by pushing us around but by working within us, his Spirit deeply and gently within us. Glory to God in the church! Glory to God in the Messiah, in Jesus! Glory down all the generations! Glory through all millennia! Oh, yes!

This is Our Monday Morning Inspiration. Let's Have a Great Week!

Dr. Willie, Apostle Paul, and the Church at Ephesus!

Scripture References:

Ephesians 3:20-21

Philippians 4:13

Let's Write!:

Reflect on the limitless power and ability of God as described in Ephesians 3:20-21. How does this truth inspire you to trust Him more fully with your hopes and dreams?

____

____

____

____

____

____

Think about a time when you experienced God's power working within you to accomplish something beyond your own ability. How did this strengthen your faith and reliance on Him?

____

____

____

____

____

22

Good Morning!

Let's start this week with praise! Say this with me: "He is exalted, the King is exalted on High. I will praise Him. He is exalted forever exalted. And I will praise His name. He is the Lord. Forever His truth shall reign. Heaven and Earth rejoice in His holy name. He is exalted, the King is exalted on high. He is exalted, the King is on High. And I will praise His name. Hallelujah! We give you glory! We give you Praise! Hallelujah!

Let's keep this energy all week long.

This is our Monday Morning Inspiration! Hallelujah! Have a Great Week!

Dr. Willie & 1 Chronicles 29:11b

Scripture References:

1 Chronicles 29:11b

Psalm 47:6-7

Let's Write!:

Reflect on the power and majesty of God as expressed in the praise song and in 1 Chronicles 29:11b. How does this inspire you to worship and praise God in your own life?

____

____

____

____

____

____

____

Think about a recent experience where you felt the presence of God through praise and worship. How did this impact your perspective and attitude for the rest of the day or week?

____

____

____

____

____

23

Good Morning!

I found the translation of Colossians 3 I was looking for to start off another great week. So here goes: "Be even-tempered, content with second place, quick to forgive an offense. Forgive as quickly and completely as the Master forgave you. And regardless of what else you put on, wear love. It's your basic, all-purpose garment. Never be without it.

Let the peace of Christ keep you in tune with each other, in step with each other. None of this going off and doing your own thing. And cultivate thankfulness.

Let the Word of Christ—the Message—have the run of the house. Give it plenty of room in your lives. Instruct and direct one another using good common sense.

And sing, sing your hearts out to God! Let every detail in your lives—words, actions, whatever—be done in the name of the Master, Jesus, thanking God the Father every step of the way!"

Dr. Willie, Apostle Paul, and Eugene Peterson's Message Translation

Scripture References:

Colossians 3:12-17

Ephesians 5:19-20

LET'S WRITE!:

Reflect on the characteristics outlined in Colossians 3:12-17 that are encouraged for believers. How can you embody these traits in your interactions with others this week?

____

____

____

____

____

____

Consider the instruction to let the Word of Christ have the run of the house and to cultivate thankfulness. How can you prioritize the Word of God and gratitude in your daily life?

____

____

____

____

____

Good Morning!

The Apostle Paul wants to exhort us on this Monday Morning with these words: "Don't run up debts, except for the huge debt of love you owe each other. When you love others, you complete what the law has been after all along. The law code—don't sleep with another person's spouse, don't take someone's life, don't take what isn't yours, don't always be wanting what you don't have, and any other "don't" you can think of—finally adds up to this: Love other people as well as you do yourself. You can't go wrong when you love others. When you add up everything in the law code, the sum total is love."

Let's go out there and have a great week!

Dr. Willie and Romans 13

Scripture References:

Romans 13:8-10

Galatians 5:14

Let's Write!:

Reflect on the concept that love fulfills the law as described in Romans 13:8-10. How can you prioritize demonstrating love in your relationships and interactions this week?

____

____

____

____

____

____

____

Consider the idea that loving others as yourself sums up the entirety of the law. How does this perspective challenge you to examine your attitudes and actions towards others?

____

____

____

____

____

____

Good Morning!

Jesus reminds his disciples on this Monday Morning that: "You didn't choose me, remember; I chose you, and put you in the world to bear fruit, fruit that won't spoil. As fruit bearers, whatever you ask the Father in relation to me, he gives you. "But remember the root command: Love one another."

Let this be our inspiration! We are chosen, to be where we are and to bring forth what will last and that's love!

Have A Great Week!

Dr. Willie and John 15

Scripture References:

John 15:16

1 Corinthians 13:13

Let's Write!:

Reflect on the idea that Jesus chose His disciples and appointed them to bear lasting fruit as described in John 15:16. How does this truth impact your understanding of your purpose and significance in God's plan?

____

____

____

____

____

____

Consider the instruction to love one another as the root command. How can you demonstrate love in practical ways to those around you this week?

____

____

____

____

26

Good Morning!

Read this with me: "It is absolutely clear that God has called "________ _______________________" (your name), to a free life. Just make sure that you don't use this freedom as an excuse to do whatever you want to do and destroy your freedom. Rather, use your freedom to serve one another in love; that's how freedom grows. For everything we know about God's Word is summed up in a single sentence: Love others as you love "_______________________," (your name). That's an act of true freedom.

Now let's go out there and Have A Great Week!

Dr. Willie and Galatians 5

Scripture References:

Galatians 5:13-14

1 Peter 2:16

Let's Write!:

Reflect on the concept of using freedom to serve one another in love as described in Galatians 5:13-14. How can you exercise your freedom in Christ to benefit others this week?

____

____

____

____

____

____

____

Consider the idea that loving others as yourself is an act of true freedom. How does this perspective challenge your understanding of freedom and responsibility in your relationships with others?

____

____

____

____

____

27

Good Morning!

As we start this new day, let us send up this simple prayer: "Lord remember me! In Jesus Name. Amen!

This is your Monday Morning Inspiration! Now let's have a Great Week!

Dr. Willie, and the Thief That Found Faith On The Cross in Luke 23.

Scripture References:

Luke 23:42-43

Psalm 25:6-7

LET'S WRITE!:

Reflect on the prayer of the thief on the cross in Luke 23:42-43. How does his simple yet profound request resonate with your own prayers and desires for God's remembrance and favor?

____

____

____

____

____

____

____

Consider the theme of remembering in Psalm 25:6-7. How does God's faithfulness to remember His people encourage you in your relationship with Him?

____

____

____

____

____

28

Good Morning!

The Amplified version of this text is here to challenge us as we start this week!

Here goes:

"If I speak with the tongues of men and of angels but have not love [for others growing out of God's love for me], then I have become only a noisy gong or a clanging cymbal [just an annoying distraction]. And if I have the gift of prophecy [and speak a new message from God to the people], and understand all mysteries, and [possess] all knowledge; and if I have all [sufficient] faith so that I can remove mountains, but do not have love [reaching out to others], I am nothing. If I give all my possessions to feed the poor, and if I surrender my body to be burned, but do not have love, it does me no good at all."

1st Corinthians 13 is our Monday Morning Inspiration. Let's be found guilty of having this kind of love.

Dr. Willie, and all the folk who will receive this Love from you!

Scripture References:

1 Corinthians 13:1-3

John 15:12

LET'S WRITE!:

Reflect on the importance of love as described in 1 Corinthians 13:1-3. How does this passage challenge your understanding of spiritual gifts, knowledge, and acts of service in relation to love?

____

____

____

____

____

____

____

Consider the commandment to love one another in John 15:12. How can you intentionally demonstrate this kind of love to those around you today?

____

____

____

____

____

Good Morning!

Let's pray: "God of our Lord Jesus the Anointed, Father of Glory: I call out to You on behalf of Your people. Give them minds ready to receive wisdom and revelation so they will truly know You. Open the eyes of their hearts, and let the light of Your truth flood in. Shine Your light on the hope You are calling them to embrace. Reveal to them the glorious riches You are preparing as their inheritance. Let them see the full extent of Your power that is at work in those of us who believe, and may it be done according to Your might and power." In Jesus Name, And It Is So, Amen!

Not only our prayer but also, our Monday Morning Inspiration.

Dr. Willie, Apostle Paul, and the Saints at Ephesus

Scripture References:

Ephesians 1:17-19

Colossians 1:9-12

Let's Write!:

Reflect on the prayer for wisdom and revelation in Ephesians 1:17-19. How does this prayer align with your own desire to know God more deeply?

____

____

____

____

____

____

____

Consider the request to understand the hope of God's calling in Colossians 1:9-12. How can you live in light of the hope and inheritance promised to believers?

____

____

____

____

____

30

Good Morning!

When it comes to cultivating relationships, Paul encourages the believers at Rome to: "Welcome with open arms fellow believers who don't see things the way you do. And don't jump all over them every time they do or say something you don't agree with—even when it seems that they are strong on opinions but weak in the faith department. Remember, they have their own history to deal with. Treat them gently."

This is Our Monday Morning Inspiration and Instructions! Let's Have a Great Week!

Dr. Willie and Romans 14

Scripture References:

Romans 14:1-3

Colossians 3:12-14

Let's Write!:

Reflect on the importance of welcoming and treating fellow believers gently as described in Romans 14:1-3. How does this attitude contribute to building unity and harmony within the body of Christ?

____

____

____

____

____

____

Consider the instruction to clothe ourselves with compassion, kindness, humility, gentleness, and patience in Colossians 3:12-14. How can you apply these virtues in your interactions with others this week?

____

____

____

____

____

31

Good Morning!

May you walk in this confidence this week!

Say to your enemies: "Your threat means nothing to us. If you throw us in the fire, the God we serve can rescue us from your roaring furnace and anything else you might cook up. But even if he doesn't, it wouldn't make a bit of difference. We still wouldn't serve your gods or worship the gold statue you set up."

Now this is our Monday Morning Inspiration! Have a great week!

Dr. Willie, Daniel, Shadrach, Meshach, and Abednego!

Scripture References:

Daniel 3:16-18

Hebrews 13:6

Let's Write!:

Reflect on the courage and trust displayed by Shadrach, Meshach, and Abednego in Daniel 3:16-18. How does their unwavering faith challenge your own trust in God's deliverance?

____

____

____

____

____

____

Consider the assurance of God's presence and protection in Hebrews 13:6. How does this promise encourage you to face challenges and opposition in your life?

____

____

____

____

____

32

Good Morning!

As we start another great week on this earth, Paul rises to encourage us with these words: "Therefore become imitators of God [copy Him and follow His example], as well-beloved children [imitate their father]; and walk continually in love [that is, value one another—practice empathy and compassion, unselfishly seeking the best for others], just as Christ also loved you and gave Himself up for us, an offering and sacrifice to God [slain for you, so that it became] a sweet fragrance."

What an opportunity we have been given to practice seeking the best for others.

This is our Monday Morning Inspiration. Let's go out there and have a great week!

Dr. Willie, Apostle Paul, and The Believers at Ephesus! -Loving & Lifting God and People

Scripture References:

Ephesians 5:1-2

1 John 3:16-18

Let's Write!:

Reflect on the call to imitate God and walk in love as described in Ephesians 5:1-2. How can you actively practice empathy, compassion, and seeking the best for others in your interactions this week?

Consider the sacrificial love demonstrated by Christ in 1 John 3:16-18. How does this love challenge you to sacrificially serve and love others in your daily life?

33

Good Morning!

Let's start this week with a simple exhortation: "Rejoice in the Lord always. I will say it again: Rejoice!"

This is our Monday Morning Inspiration. Now let's have a Great Week!

Dr. Willie, Apostle Paul, and The Holy Ghost that told me "Everything Gonna Be Alright!"

Scripture References:

Philippians 4:4

Psalm 118:24

LET'S WRITE!:

Reflect on the command to rejoice always in Philippians 4:4. How can you cultivate a spirit of joy even amidst challenges or difficulties this week?

____

____

____

____

____

____

Consider the reminder to rejoice in Psalm 118:24. How does this verse

encourage you to approach each day with gratitude and joy in the Lord?

____

____

____

____

____

34

Good Morning!

God is strong, and he wants you strong. So, take everything the Master has set out for you, well-made weapons of the best materials. And put them to use so you will be able to stand up to everything the Devil throws your way.

This is your Monday Morning Inspiration! You are equipped and ready for total victory!

Let's Have A Great Week...

Dr. Willie and The Church at Ephesus.

Scripture References:

Ephesians 6:10-11

2 Corinthians 10:4-5

Let's Write!:

Reflect on the imagery of spiritual warfare in Ephesians 6:10-11. How can you actively engage in using the spiritual weapons God has provided to stand firm against the enemy's schemes?

____

____

____

____

____

____

____

Consider the concept of taking every thought captive in 2 Corinthians 10:4-5. How can you apply this principle in your daily life to guard your mind and stand strong in faith?

____

____

____

____

____

35

Good Morning!

Hebrews rises this morning to encourage us with these words: "Let us hold unswervingly to the hope we profess, for He who promised is faithful."

Yes! Faithful is the One who promised! So don't give up. Hold On!!

This is Our Monday Morning Inspiration.

Now Let's Have A Great Week!

Dr. Willie and Hebrews

Scripture References:

Hebrews 10:23

Lamentations 3:22-23

LET'S WRITE!:

Reflect on the concept of holding unswervingly to hope as mentioned in Hebrews 10:23. How does this assurance of God's faithfulness impact your perspective during challenging times?

____

____

____

____

____

____

____

Consider the idea of God's faithfulness enduring forever in Lamentations 3:22-23. How does this truth influence your trust in God's promises for your life?

____

____

____

____

____

36

Good Morning!

I found the translation of Colossians 3 I was looking for to start off another great week.

So here goes: "Be even-tempered, content with second place, quick to forgive an offense. Forgive as quickly and completely as the Master forgave you. And regardless of what else you put on, wear love. It's your basic, all-purpose garment. Never be without it.

Let the peace of Christ keep you in tune with each other, in step with each other. None of this going off and doing your own thing. And cultivate thankfulness.

Let the Word of Christ—the Message—have the run of the house. Give it plenty of room in your lives. Instruct and direct one another using good common sense.

And sing, sing your hearts out to God! Let every detail in your lives—words, actions, whatever—be done in the name of the Master, Jesus, thanking God the Father every step of the way!"

Dr. Willie, Apostle Paul, and Eugene Peterson's Message Translation

Scripture References:

Colossians 3:12-17

Ephesians 5:20

Let's Write!:

Reflect on the importance of forgiveness as described in Colossians 3:13. How does forgiving others align with the forgiveness we receive from God?

Consider the instruction to let the Word of Christ have the run of the house in Colossians 3:16. How can you prioritize the Word of God in your daily life and decision-making?

37

Good Morning!

This is a season of Prophetic Happenings! This is the time where you we SEE what was spoken to you by God Almighty. Whatever the leap is that you need to take.... Take It... Whatever move that you need to make... Make It.... This Gospel is not only for the people who hear it, it's for the one Who Preaches It... No more feeling left out of the Harvest.... It's Also Your Time.... Miracles, Signs and Wonders, not only through you, BUT FOR YOU... Yes, it's early... But I had to tell you what I just saw and heard.... Doors, wells, rivers, lands and more.... And peace... I just heard the Sound of more Prophetic Happenings....

I'm praying for you and with you! Have a Great Weekend/Year-end in life and Ministry...!

Happy Preaching!

Dr. Willie and The Sounds of Heaven.

Scripture References:

Isaiah 43:18-19

Joel 2:28

Let's Write!:

Reflect on a time when you felt a strong sense of God's leading or a prophetic revelation. How did you respond to it, and what were the outcomes?

____

____

____

____

____

____

____

Consider the concept of being part of the harvest in ministry. How can you actively participate in the work of God's kingdom in your community or sphere of influence?

____

____

____

____

____

38

Good Morning!

As we look toward a strong finish for this year, Tyler Perry rises today to exhort us to "Trust God and Do What Is Good."

This is our Monday Morning Inspiration. Now let's go and Have A Great Week!

Dr. Willie and Tyler

Scripture References:

Psalm 37:3

Proverbs 3:5-6

Let's Write!:

How do you define "doing what is good" in your life? Reflect on instances where trusting God led you to do what is good.

____

____

____

____

____

____

____

In what areas of your life do you find it challenging to trust God completely? How can you cultivate a deeper sense of trust and reliance on God in those areas?

____

____

____

____

____

____

39

Good Morning!

The Wisdom of Solomon rises to instruct us with these words: "Live wisely and wisdom will permeate your life; mock life and life will mock you."

Save your breath for the wise—they'll be wiser for it; tell good people what you know—they'll profit from it. Skilled living gets its start in the Fear-of-God, insight into life from knowing a Holy God. It's through me, Lady Wisdom, that your life deepens, and the years of your life ripen.

This is our Monday Morning Inspiration! Let's Have a Great Week!

Dr. Willie and Proverbs 9

Scripture References:

Proverbs 1:7

Proverbs 9:10

Let's Write!:

How do you prioritize seeking wisdom in your daily life? Reflect on how you've seen wisdom positively impact your decisions and actions.

____

____

____

____

____

____

____

In what ways can you actively cultivate a deeper reverence for God in your pursuit of wisdom? How might this enhance your understanding of life and your relationships?

____

____

____

____

____

____

Good Morning!

The Epistle of Peter exhorts us to, "Be sober [well balanced and self-disciplined], be alert and cautious at all times. That enemy of yours, the devil, prowls around like a roaring lion [fiercely hungry], seeking someone to devour. But resist him, be firm in your faith [against his attack—rooted, established, immovable], knowing that the same experiences of suffering are being experienced by your brothers and sisters throughout the world. [You do not suffer alone.]

BUT...!!!!!!!

After you have suffered for a little while, the God of all grace [who imparts His blessing and favor], who called you to His own eternal glory in Christ, will Himself complete, confirm, strengthen, and establish you [making you what you ought to be]. To Him be dominion (power, authority, sovereignty) forever and ever. Amen.

Wow. This is Our Monday Morning Inspiration! Let's Have A Great Week!

Dr. Willie and The Epistle of Peter!

Scripture References:

1 Peter 5:8-10

2 Peter 1:10-11

LET'S WRITE!:

How do you maintain spiritual vigilance in the face of adversity and spiritual attacks? Reflect on practical ways to strengthen your faith and resist temptation.

____

____

____

____

____

____

In what ways have you experienced the transformative power of God's grace during times of suffering or trial? Reflect on how these experiences have shaped your character and deepened your trust in God's faithfulness.

____

____

____

____

Good Morning!

Have you read Psalm 126, that talks about when God brings you out of one of the toughest seasons of your life? No? Here Goes!

"It seemed like a dream, too good to be true, when God returned Zion's exiles. We laughed, we sang, we couldn't believe our good fortune. We were the talk of the nations—SEP "God was wonderful to them!" God was wonderful to us; we are one happy people. And now, God, do it again— bring rains to our drought-stricken lives, So those who planted their crops in despair will shout "Yes!" at the harvest, So those who went off with heavy hearts will come home laughing, with armloads of blessing."

See That! You Will Have Armloads of Blessing!

This is our Monday Morning Inspiration! Have a Great Week!

Dr. Willie, Ezra & The People of God

Scripture References:

Psalm 126:1-6

Ezra 9:8-9

Let's Write!:

Reflect on a time when you experienced God's deliverance from a challenging situation. How did it feel to witness His faithfulness and restoration?

____

____

____

____

____

____

____

In what areas of your life do you currently need God's intervention and blessing? Take some time to pray and express your hopes and desires for His provision and guidance.

____

____

____

____

____

Good Morning!

Every time your name comes up in my prayers, I say, "Oh, thank you, God!" I keep hearing of the love and faith you have for the Master Jesus, which brims over to other believers. And I keep praying that this faith we hold in common keeps showing up in the good things we do, and that people recognize Christ in all of it.

Friend, you have no idea how good your love makes me realize how much Christ loves us all, doubly so when I see your hospitality to fellow believers.

On this Monday Morning, Be Inspired to Keep Going and Keep Loving! And that love will lead us all to a Great Week!

Have a Good One!

Dr. Willie, Apostle Paul, and all who will experience your forgiveness and grace this week!

Scripture References:

Philemon 1:4-7

1 John 4:7-8

Let's Write!:

Reflect on a time when someone's love and faith deeply impacted you. How did it affect your relationship with God and others?

____

____

____

____

____

____

____

How can you demonstrate Christ's love and hospitality to others in your daily interactions this week? Consider practical ways to extend forgiveness, grace, and kindness to those around you.

____

____

____

____

____

43

Good Morning!

Isn't it obvious that God deliberately chose men and women that the culture overlooks and exploits and abuses, chose these "nobodies" to expose the hollow pretensions of the "somebodies"? That makes it quite clear that none of us can get by with blowing our own horn before God. Everything that we have—right thinking and right living, a clean slate, and a fresh start—comes from God by way of Jesus Christ. That's why we have the saying, "If you're going to blow a horn, blow a trumpet for God."

Well, that about says it! This is Our Monday Morning Inspiration from Paul's letter to Corinth. Let's go out and Have A Great Week!

Dr. Willie & Apostle Paul

Scripture References:

1 Corinthians 1:26-31

Romans 11:36

Let's Write!:

Reflect on a time when you felt undervalued or overlooked by society. How did that experience shape your perspective on God's value system?

____

____

____

____

____

____

In what ways can you actively "blow a trumpet for God" in your daily life? Consider how you can use your talents and resources to uplift and serve others in alignment with God's purposes.

____

____

____

____

____

____

Good Morning!

Apostle Peter rises to share with us these words: "Friends, this world is not your home, so don't make yourselves cozy in it. Don't indulge your ego at the expense of your soul. Live an exemplary life in your neighborhood so that your actions will refute their prejudices. Then they'll be won over to God's side and be there to join in the celebration when he arrives."

Wow! What a charge for our Monday Morning Inspiration. Let's have A Great Week!

Dr. Willie and Apostle Peter

Scripture References:

1 Peter 2:11-12

Philippians 3:20

Let's Write!:

How do you maintain a balance between engaging with the world around you and remembering that your true home is in heaven?

____

____

____

____

____

____

Reflect on a time when your actions had a positive impact on someone else's perception of God. How did this experience encourage or challenge you in your faith journey?

____

____

____

____

____

____

Good Morning!

Galatians tells us, "This is the way it was with us before Christ came. We were slaves to Jewish laws and rituals, for we thought they could save us. But when the right time came, the time God decided on, he sent his Son, born of a woman, born as a Jew, to buy freedom for us who were slaves to the law so that he could adopt us as his very own sons. And because we are his sons, God has sent the Spirit of his Son into our hearts, so now we can rightly speak of God as our dear Father. Now we are no longer slaves but God's own sons and daughters. And since we are his sons, everything he has belongs to us, for that is the way God planned." And I'm open for God's Plan!

This is Our Monday Morning Inspiration and I pray you have a great week!

Dr. Willie, Apostle Paul, Dr. Jon, Holy Spirit, and Mary The Mother of Jesus!

Scripture References:

Galatians 4:3-7

Romans 8:15

LET'S WRITE!:

Reflect on a time when you felt the freedom and joy of being a child of God. How did this experience shape your understanding of your relationship with Him?

In what ways can you actively embrace God's plan for your life this week, trusting in His guidance and provision?

Good Morning!

"What marvelous love the Father has extended to us! Just look at it—we're called children of God! That's who we really are. But that's also why the world doesn't recognize us or take us seriously, because it has no idea who he is or what he's up to.

But friends, that's exactly who we are: children of God. And that's only the beginning. Who knows how we'll end up!

What we know is that when Christ is openly revealed, we'll see him—and in seeing him, become like him.

All of us who look forward to his Coming stay ready, with the glistening purity of Jesus' life as a model for our own."

This is Our Monday Morning Inspiration, now Let's Have A Great Week!

Dr. Willie and John The Apostle

Scripture References:

1 John 3:1-3

1 Corinthians 13:12

LET'S WRITE!:

How does knowing that you are a child of God impact the way you navigate challenges and uncertainties in life?

____

____

____

____

____

____

Reflect on a time when you experienced personal growth in your faith journey, becoming more like Jesus. What contributed to that growth, and how can you continue to emulate Jesus in your daily life?

____

____

____

____

____

Good Morning!

"It's time for our Monday Morning Inspiration and it comes from Proverbs 21:21!

Solomon says, 'Whoever goes hunting for what is right and kind finds life itself—glorious life!'

I'm ready for more of what's right, kind and life itself. Let's make it a great week!

Dr. Willie, King Solomon, The Holy Ghost, and Life Itself."

Scripture References:

Proverbs 21:21

Matthew 6:33

Let's Write!:

Reflect on a recent experience where you actively pursued what is right and kind. How did it impact your own sense of fulfillment and well-being?

____

____

____

____

____

____

____

Consider how you can incorporate the pursuit of righteousness and kindness into your daily life this week. What specific actions or attitudes can you cultivate to align with these values?

____

____

____

____

____

Good Morning!

"If you ever get in trouble, David rises this morning to share with us his plea to God. David says, 'I run for dear life to God, I'll never live to regret it. Do what you do so well: get me out of this mess and up on my feet. Put your ear to the ground and listen, give me space for salvation. Be a guest room where I can retreat; you (God) said your door was always open! You're my salvation—my vast, granite fortress.'

This is some good useable news on this Monday Morning... Be Inspired and Let's Have A Great Week!

Dr. Willie, David of Psalm 71, and Our Vast Granite Fortress."

Scripture References:

Psalm 71:1-3

Psalm 91:2

LET'S WRITE!:

Reflect on a time when you turned to God for help in a difficult situation. How did you experience His presence and protection?

____

____

____

____

____

Consider the ways in which you can cultivate a deeper reliance on God as your fortress and refuge in your daily life. How can you make space for God to be your strength and salvation?

____

____

____

____

____

____

Good Morning!

"John the Elder rises to encourage us with these words: 'Let's not just talk about love; let's practice real love. This is the only way we'll know we're living truly, living in God's reality. It's also the way to shut down debilitating self-criticism, even when there is something to it. For God is greater than our worried hearts and knows more about us than we do ourselves.'

This God reality thing is the real deal and it's a great theme for our Monday Morning Inspiration! Now be blessed and Have a Great Week!

Dr. Willie, God Omniscient, and John (1st John 3)"

Scripture References:

1 John 3:18

1 John 3:20

LET'S WRITE!:

Reflect on a time when you demonstrated real love in action. How did this experience impact your understanding of living in God's reality?

____

____

____

____

____

____

____

Consider any self-critical thoughts you may have had recently. How can you apply the truth that God knows and loves you deeply to combat these thoughts and live with greater confidence in His grace?

____

____

____

____

____

____

Good Morning!

As we embark on a new week, let us draw wisdom from the words of Moses, who reminds us of the importance of discerning between the good and the God-ordained. Sometimes, challenges arise to test our faith and commitment to God. Moses emphasizes the need to love and follow God wholeheartedly, holding Him in reverence, obeying His commandments, and serving Him with unwavering devotion.

This Monday Morning Inspiration serves as a reminder to stay steadfast in our faith and trust in God's guidance. Let us not be swayed by the distractions of the world but remain firmly rooted in our devotion to Him.

Now, as we step into this week, let's embrace the challenges with courage and faith, knowing that we are held by the loving hand of our Creator.

Have an Amazing Week!

Dr. Willie, Moses, and All The Children of God

Scripture References:

Deuteronomy 13:4

James 1:12

Let's Write!:

How do you discern between what is merely good and what is truly aligned with God's will in your life?

____

____

____

____

____

____

____

Reflect on a time when you faced a challenge that tested your faith. How did you respond, and what did you learn from the experience?

____

____

____

____

____

____

51

Good Morning!

As we start this new week, let's draw inspiration from the wisdom of the Apostle Paul as expressed in the book of Hebrews. Paul reminds us not to be consumed by the pursuit of material possessions but to find contentment in what we already have. With the assurance of God's unfailing presence and support, we can confidently declare our fearlessness in the face of any challenge.

This Monday Morning Inspiration encourages us to shift our focus from worldly desires to trust in God's provision and protection. When we fully rely on Him, we can navigate life with boldness and confidence, knowing that nothing can shake our faith.

So, as we embark on this week's journey, let's carry this assurance in our hearts and face whatever comes our way with unwavering courage.

Have a Great Week!

Dr. Willie, The Apostle Paul, and the Fearless People of God

Scripture References:

Hebrews 13:5-6

Philippians 4:12-13

Let's Write!:

How do you typically find contentment in your life, especially in times of need or want?

____

____

____

____

____

____

Reflect on a moment when you felt God's presence and support, giving you the courage to face a difficult situation. How did this experience impact your faith journey?

____

____

____

____

____

52

Good Morning!

As we embark on a new week, let's heed the words of John the Apostle, who reminds us of the importance of aligning our actions with our faith. Claiming to know God is not enough; true intimacy with Him is demonstrated through obedience to His commandments and living a life that reflects His love.

This Monday Morning Inspiration calls us to authenticity and integrity in our relationship with God. It challenges us to examine whether our actions align with our profession of faith and if our lives bear witness to the transformative power of God's love.

So, as we step into this week, let's commit to living in a manner that reflects the character of Christ. Let's strive to walk in obedience to God's word and embody His love in all that we do.

Have a Great Week!

Dr. Willie, John The Apostle, and The Holy Spirit

Scripture References:

1 John 2:4-6

John 14:15

Let's Write!:

Reflect on a time when your actions did not align with your faith. What steps can you take to ensure greater consistency between your beliefs and your behavior?

____

____

____

____

____

____

____

Consider how your life reflects the love of Christ to others. In what ways can you further demonstrate God's love in your daily interactions and relationships?

____

____

____

____

____

____

RESOURCES

Holy Bible, King James Version (KJV)

MEET DR. WILLIE THOMPSON

Dr. Willie Thompson, a native of Columbia, South Carolina, is a distinguished scholar and leader deeply committed to the betterment of communities. He earned his Baccalaureate Degree in Religion & Philosophy from Benedict College, and subsequently pursued higher education, earning both his Master of Divinity and Doctor of Philosophy from Howard University in Washington, D.C.

As an accomplished author, entrepreneur, and executive coach, Dr. Thompson is widely recognized as a sought-after thought leader in his field. He has dedicated his career to empowering individuals and communities through education and outreach initiatives. Dr. Thompson is the visionary founder of two impactful non-profit religious organizations, which are dedicated to fostering empowerment and growth.

Driven by his passion for research and writing, Dr. Thompson is currently preparing to share his insights with the global community. His forthcoming publications will address the vital topic of nurturing faith communities amidst the challenges of contemporary society, offering valuable guidance to those seeking to uphold sacred values in a rapidly changing world.

In addition to his academic and literary pursuits, Dr. Thompson is an active member of Kappa Alpha Psi Fraternity, Inc., embodying the principles of service and leadership in all aspects of his life. He serves as an Assistant Professor of Interdisciplinary Studies, Research, and Religion at Benedict College, where he imparts his knowledge and wisdom to the next generation of leaders.

Dr. Thompson's commitment to spiritual leadership extends to his role as the senior servant and pastor of Oak Grove Baptist Church in Pontiac, South Carolina. Through his dynamic leadership, he inspires and guides his congregation with compassion and dedication.

With his wealth of experience, profound insights, and unwavering dedication to his calling, Dr. Willie Thompson continues to make a profound impact on individuals and communities alike, leaving a lasting legacy of empowerment, education, and spiritual growth.